Old PERTH

by

GUTHRIE HUTTON

The size of their works and the risk of fire from chemicals meant that Pullar's had their own fire brigade, based in Kinnoul Street. It also helped at fires in the city and the city brigade reciprocated by helping them; notably in March 1903 when a major disaster in the benzine washing machine room was averted by their combined efforts.

First Published in the United Kingdom, 1995
By Richard Stenlake, Ochiltree Sawmill, The Lade, Ochiltree, Ayrshire KA18 2NX
Telephone: 01290 700266

ISBN 1-872074-48-0

An unidentified shop interior with sweetie jars that appear to come from Campbell's of Feus Road. The connection with the town is clear, but the prominently displayed McDowell's biscuits come from Edinburgh, so is the shop in Perth or somewhere else?

INTRODUCTION

Perth seemed to almost burst out of its mediaeval confines in the late eighteenth and early nineteenth centuries. The city gates (or ports) were knocked down to ease traffic flow, new, broad, elegant streets were created and a new bridge was built across the Tay. That bridge ended 150 years of cross river isolation and heralded a new era of prosperity for the town.

Before that time, little had changed. Perth was a tightly packed warren of closes, wynds and vennels leading off narrow crooked streets. Densely packed buildings occupied every inch of ground behind the old town walls. A remarkable system of lades fed water from the River Almond around the town to drive its mills and provide water for other needs. The castle, destroyed by a flood in 1209, was never rebuilt and so the town was dominated by four monasteries and its church. It was dedicated to Saint John the Baptist and gave Perth its alternative name; Saint John's Toun.

It was an important town too, in effect the early Capital of Scotland. The parliament met in Perth and Scottish Kings were crowned at Scone. One of those Kings, James I, was murdered in Perth, while another, James VI, escaped a similar fate. An earlier King, Robert III, had sought to settle a long running feud between the warring Highland Clans, Chattan and Kay, by having thirty men from each fight to the death on the North Inch; a bloody butchery that formed the background to Sir Walter Scott's novel the Fair Maid of Perth. In 1559, with resentment at the greedy and overbearing church establishment already running high, the prominent reformer John Knox delivered a sermon that started a riot. The people of Perth went on an orgy of looting and destruction that lasted two days, the monasteries and church were stripped of valuables and food and their 'idolatrous images' burned and broken. It was the start of the Reformation.

But murdering Kings, fighting on the Inch and religious riots were all part of the old Perth that the eighteenth century enlightenment swept away like a Tay flood. And if that was the catalyst then railways were the key that allowed Perth to take advantage of its superb position in the centre of the country at the first practical crossing point and navigable limit of the Tay. Tracks radiated in all directions allowing for the rapid development of industry and finance in the nineteenth century.

Dye works and dry cleaning, weaving and whisky, insurance and agriculture, salmon and bull sales all combined to sweep Perth into the twentieth century on a wave of prosperity and optimism. The outward spread of the built up area, encouraged first by trams and then by buses, absorbed outlying areas so that now the old mediaeval burgh is just the core at the centre of a large thriving county town. And those buses, the core of another business success.

Yet amidst the optimism there is a cloud; but one with a silver lining. The absence of a bridge for 150 years stifled the local economy, and the sudden release of finance and energy started a relentless process of renewal. Much that would be prized today was lost, but with the beautiful restoration of the Lower City Mills powered by water from the lade, and the retention of the water works and the old hospital frontage for the A.K.Bell Library, there are indications that new Perth has begun to appreciate the value of the old.

Guthrie Hutton, July 1995

High Street was the main street running through old Perth to the original bridge and has remained at the centre of life in the town ever since. This picture shows it around 1890 before King Edward Street was built. It was taken by one of Scotland's leading early photographers George Washington Wilson, or by one of his sons who maintained his documentary traditions into the twentieth century. King Edward Sreet joined High Street where the cart is parked on the left, just beyond the 'boot' shop sign of R & A Wilson's boot and shoe makers'. Opposite the 'boot', on the right hand side of the street, a man is standing, with a Thomas Cook sign above him, at the mouth of Guard Vennel. One of the shops just beyond Guard Vennel was John Dewar's wine and spirit merchants business; the humble beginnings of Dewar's whisky.

Dewar's shop site was redeveloped in 1925 by F.W.Woolworths as their first shop in Perth, seen here in 1939. Wallace's 'Store of Satisfaction' is on the King Edward Street corner, on the left, with 'tickety' Macdonald's further up the street. Saint Paul's church steeple is prominient at the top of High Street and the crowds of cars show what it was like before it was pedestrianised. It is interesting to compare this picture with the previous one. Redevelopment, and the building of King Edward Street, have greatly altered the street in the fifty years between the pictures and a comparison with High Street of today shows that the process has continued. Few of the older buildings seen here now remain, including Woolworths who redeveloped their site again in 1966. Guard Vennel is on the extreme right beside Woolies.

This is not a picture by one of the great photographic pioneers but it is still a priceless gem showing High Street about 1900. In the distance, on the right, is a low building which is now the site of another of High Street's big stores, Marks and Spencer. They allowed a major archaeologial excavation, when the site was redeveloped in the 1970's, which uncovered valuable information about mediaeval Perth. The pedestrians on the left are crossing the end of Saint John Street with the opening of Kirkgate further up on the left and Skinnergate on the right. They formed the main north-south axis through the old town and the mercat cross was in High Street at its intersection with them. The first cross was demolished in 1651 by Oliver Cromwell's soldiers and its replacement was removed in 1764, when it became an impediment to traffic.

Watergate was mediaeval Perth's most prestigious streeet with large houses and gardens running down to the Tay. It was the first street in the town to be paved with cut stones, rather than river stones. It quickly lost its importance and amenity however when Tay Street was laid out in the nineteenth century cutting the gardens of its houses off from the riverside; it was clearly no longer the top people's street when a night shelter for itinerant female workers was opened in 1901. In 1651 Oliver Cromwell negotiated the surrender of the town in the Watergate house of a leading citizen, John Davidson. His irritation at the presence of this uninvited guest, turned to anger when the side wall of his house fell down, not so much because it had fallen, but because Cromwell had left just before it fell.

The finest of the Watergate houses was the sixteenth century Gowrie House, home of the Earls of Gowrie. It is seen here looking from South Street and if it was still standing would contribute greatly to Perth's heritage; but South Street, and the view on the next page, would be very different. One of Scotland's great unsolved mysteries occurred within its walls when King James VI apparently escaped assassination and the Earl of Gowrie and his brother were killed, but who had plottted against who and was it murder or a successful defence of the King? The town presented the house to the Duke of Cumberland in 1746. He promptly sold it to the Government who used it as a barracks until Perth Barracks were built. It was demolished in 1809. In the background, between the trees on the right, are the masts of a sailing ship on the Tay.

The other main east - west street in mediaeval times was South Street, seen here in the early 1960's with Saint John Street on the left. On the right is the Salutation Hotel, claimed to be the oldest Inn in Scotland. It dates back to 1699 and also boasts being where Bonnie Prince Charlie stayed when his Jacobite army stopped in Perth in 1745. At that time South Street stopped at what was then a T-junction with Watergate and Speygate, giving it a view of the Gowrie House and not, as here, across the Tay. Access to the river was only created in the early nineteenth century and South Street became a main through route when Victoria Bridge was opened in 1900. The regular building line and busy one-way traffic (in which all of these cars would be booked for going the wrong way!) have now robbed the street of much of its character.

Gowrie House was demolished to make way for the County Court Buildings which were erected on the site in 1820, out of this picture on the left. It was the beginning of the end for Watergate and the beginnings of the development of the riverside. The Tay Street buildings on the left, dating from the 1870's, also saw the beginnings of General Accident Fire and Life Assurance Corporation. It was from here, at number 44, that the small local concern grew under the direction of its far sighted manager Francis (later Sir Francis) Norie-Miller into a large Corporation. The offices moved to the corner of Tay Street and High Street in 1901, but the original premises were retained and are still used as a company archive. In the right foreground is the end of Victoria Bridge which was opened in 1900 but replaced by Queen's Bridge in 1960.

Perth's bridges suffered historically from having the misfortune of being built across the swift and turbulent Tay. One was destroyed in 1209, another late in the sixteenth century and its replacement was swept away in 1621 only a few years after it was completed. Perth lost faith in bridges after that and was unable to raise the money for a new one. For 150 years cross river traffic went by ferry, an unsatisfactory state of affairs that was brought to an end when John Smeaton, famous as the builder of the Forth and Clyde Canal, built the new Perth Bridge, opened in 1771. Smeaton took no chances and designed a bridge that was so strong it was able to be widened a hundred years later and then have tram tracks laid across it. The circular apertures between the arches were designed to allow flood water through, but were found to be unnecessary and bricked up.

The new bridge was not aligned with the High Street as the previous bridges had been and so George Street was cut through some of the old town in the late eighteenth century, to provide a link from the town centre. In the distance is the Museum and Art Gallery. The first part of the building, the domed rotunda, was erected as a memorial to Lord Provost, Thomas Hay Marshall in 1822 and it was extended in the 1930's. It houses an excellent collection, enhanced by finds from the High Street and other excavations. George Street itself was the site of an excavtion in 1968. This picture taken in the 1930's shows the tram lines still in place, but instead of a tram, a bus is weaving its way through the traffic apparently on the old tram route from Scone to Cherrybank. The last tram service ran over these tracks in 1928.

Saint John Street was driven through the old town at the same time as George Street, to provide better access from the Edinburgh Road to the new bridge. Part of it was on the line of the old Salt Vennel and its proximity to the kirk meant that it opened up the heart of the mediaeval burgh. Saint John's Church, on the left here, is Perth's only surviving building of any antiquity. The building opposite was the head office of Perth's Central Bank, which was established in 1834 and remained independent until taken over by the Bank of Scotland in 1868. The car on the left is outside what was Fenwick's bakers and confectioners shop and where the man is was Mathieson the butchers. On the right, on the corner with South Street, was Andrew Laing's grocers and wine merchants shop and on the opposite corner was Kennoway's bakers shop and restaurant.

When the City Hall, on the left, was opened in 1911 the Lord Provost declared that it would 'remain for centuries' - there are now proposals to demolish it! It was built to replace its smaller predecessor which itself had been opened in 1845. It has become famous in more recent years as the venue for political party conferences. In front of it here is the twentieth century version of the town's mercat cross, which was erected in 1913 and surrounded by these gardens in Saint John's Square as a memorial to King Edward VII. On the left, behind the mercat cross, is Valentines Buildings, put up before the First World War by Valentines Motors Ltd. They were one of Perth's earliest motor dealers who started hiring charabancs and were latterly agents for Austin cars and trucks. The Salvation Army citadel is on the corner with South Street.

The corner of Valentines Buildings is on the extreme left of this view of Saint John's Square, (or as Valentines Motors called it 'City Hall Square'). It was a typical shops, offices and housing 'precinct' of the early 1960's, a period when many of Scotland's decaying town centres were revitalised by wholesale demolition and rebuilding rather than by restoration. Like so many others, the flaws in its utopian post war planning were quickly exposed and, in a relatively short time, it has been replaced by the Saint John's Centre, itself a typical shops, offices and housing development of the 1990's. Valentines buildings were demolished to make way for it, but the mercat cross has survived through all the unheaval. Until the 1970's, the City Fire Brigade was based in King Edward Street, just out of picture on the right.

Perth Theatre opened in 1900, but its golden period was when Marjorie Dence and David Steuart took it over in 1935. Three years later they received a Royal Command to perform for King George VI and Queen Elizabeth at Balmoral. After the War, on 29th May 1951, their daughter Princess Elizabeth, two years before she was crowned Queen, repayed the compliment when she came to Perth to see this peformance of Shakespeare's Twelth Night, staged as part of the Festival of Britain. The Princess met the cast on stage after the show. I remember the production well; my mother, who had worked for a London theatrical costumiers before the Second World War, worked on the costumes for it and took my brother, sister and myself to see the dress rehearsal. But, at the tender age of nine, I preferred the pantomimes - more laughs!

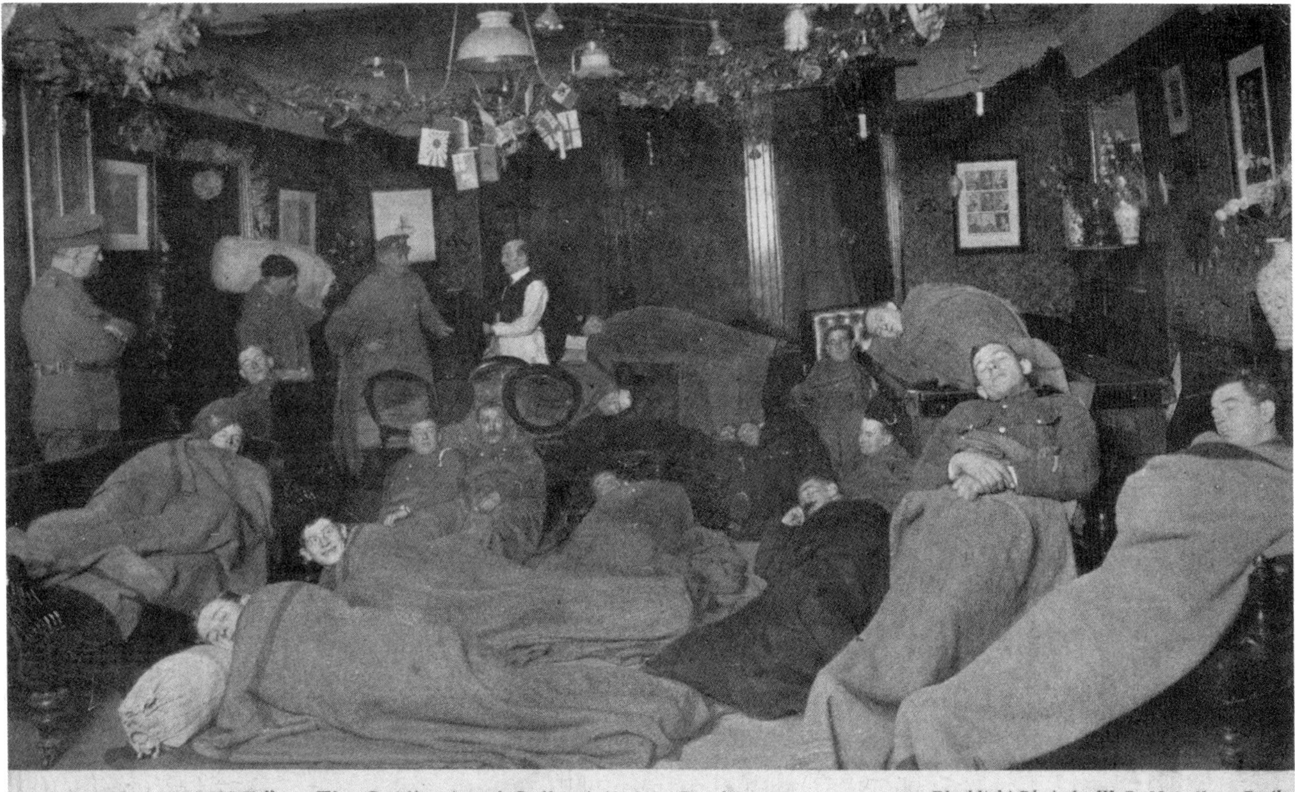

"A FULL HOUSE." The Soldiers' and Sailors' Home, Perth. *Flashlight Photo by W. B. McCallum, Perth.*

A 'full house' is of course a theatre manager's dream, although this scene of somnolent soldiery would probably be more like a nightmare audience. Being at a railway crossroads, many servicemen will have found themselves in Perth looking for a bed for the night, or just simply looking for a place to lay their head, like here where every available space, including the billiard table, has been taken up, as yet more men arrive. The room appears to be seasonally decorated so no doubt the men are heading home on Christmas leave. The location of this flashlit interior could be at 30/32 York Place where there was a Soldiers' and Sailors' home at the time of the First World War. Alternatively it could have been at 25 Scott Street where the words 'Soldiers' Home' can still be seen painted on the gable wall and 'welcome' is above the door.

W.B.McCallum, who took the photograph on the previous page, had a shop just across the road at No.8 Scott Street. It is still a photographic shop. The soldiers' home was originally the Wauchope and Black Watch Memorial Home and can be seen on the left of this picture looking north from South Street around 1900. It is the large tenement next to the prominent buildings with classical pediment and dome. They have been demolished. The southern end of Scott Street was another Georgian period street running from the South Inch to Canal Street, where the old city walls and town lade marked the limit of the mediaeval town. It was extended north through the old town in the late nineteenth century. The shop on the right here, on the corner with South Street, was William Paton's pastry bakery and tea room.

The prominent building on the left of this 1930's picture looking north along Kinnoul Street, is the Sandeman Library, opened in 1898. The building and books were paid for out of a bequest of £30,000 from Professor Archibald Sandeman of Cambridge University, hence the name. The library has now been moved to York Place, but no longer bears the Sandeman name. Opposite the Congregational Church, on the right hand side of the street, is the works of the dyers and dry cleaners, John Pullar and Sons. Next to it, nearer to camera, is Bordeaux House, a name which betrays the wine shipping origins of another of Perth's famous whisky names, Matthew Gloag and Sons. The car in the left foreground bears the old Perthshire vehicle registration plate of ES. The other car is from Paisley.

By the end of the eighteenth century printing and dyeing was an established industry in Perth. The most successful company, John Pullar and Sons, started with a staff of six and grew to employ around 2000 people in the extensive works behind these old tenements. When this picture was taken, around 1905, Pullars had become known throughout Britain for dry cleaning. The works were built in this crowded part of the town, so that they could use water from the town lade, which ran beneath them. The uniform bulk of the works here is in marked contrast to the random old buildings in front. The irregular triangle of cobbled streets around them was, to the left Carpenter Street, to the right Union Street and behind them, Cherry Lane. They disappeared long ago and the site is now planted with trees and cars - both just seem to grow!

This close-up of Cherry Lane, at the back of the triangle on the previous page, shows how closely packed these old buildings were, with stairs giving access to houses set at all levels and angles to them. The house on the right, in Mill Wynd (although seen here from the back lane), was said by Sir Walter Scott to be the home of Hal o' The Wynd, an historical character made famous in his novel the Fair Maid of Perth. Hal's moment of fame came in the clan battle in 1396 when one of the Clan Chattan (wisely) thought the better of it, jumped into the Tay, and escaped. Hal (unwisely) took his place for half a French gold dollar, but unlike most of the clansmen he survived to spend it. The house, near the restored Lower City Mills, is now incorporated into the South Methven Street branch of the Clydesdale Bank.

The old city wall ran behind the buildings on the left of this view of South Methven Street. At its junction with South Street was the South Street Port, one of the main gates in the wall. All of the gates were removed in 1764, at the same time as the town cross. At the base of the wall was a road which followed its irregular curving line and which was straightened out when South Methven Street was created. Tucked in behind the prominent tenement on the right hand side of this picture from the 1900's however, are two buildings set at an angle that is almost certainly a throwback to the line of the old road. The same buildings can be seen alongside John Moir's pub on the back cover. The tenement replaced the pub building, but at least kept up the tradition by having the Central Bar on the ground floor. It is still a pub, but with a different name.

Half hidden behind the trees on the right hand side of this 1930's picture of York Place is the building that was first opened as the County and City Infirmary in 1836. It continued as the main hospital for the area until 1914, when the Perth Royal Infirmary was opened, but it remained in use as a Red Cross Hospital during the First World War. The building was later used as the headquarters of Perth County Council and the frontage has now been successfully incorporated into a new building for the A.K.Bell Library, which has replaced the Sandeman Library. The sign on the gable of the tenement on the left hand side of the picture, indicates the popular York House Restaurant below, it too has a new name. Out of picture on the left is the twin turreted Free Church building, now used by the Church of the Nazarene (see page 56).

Perth's central location made it strategically important to numerous railway companies who were poised to come in just as soon as the Town Council agreed to a site for the station. The debate centred on whether or not to use the South Inch, but that idea was eventually squashed and the station opened on the present site in 1848. It was extended in 1866 and completely re-built in 1886 when the original buildings were submerged in the middle of an enlarged structure. The curved platforms for the Dundee line were also added at this time. The original buildings are on the right of this main north - south island platform which is over 1700 feet long and is seen here at a time when, on the arrival of an Inverness train in July or August, it could be '... so crowded with passengers, parcels and luggage that there was scarcely room to move'.

The station was built by the Scottish Central Railway which had become part of the Caledonian Railway when these pictures were taken around the time of the First World War. Here, Caley locomotive No. 117 waits to head south with the London 'Postal'. She was built in 1912 as one of a small class of super-heated engines. They had low coal and water consumption and were ideal for services, like the 'Postal', which could have engines running 150 miles from Perth to Carlisle without taking on water. Many other railway companies used the station, but after amalgamations in 1923 there were only two, the L.M.S. and L.N.E.R. Both had separate workshops and marshalling yards, making the railways one of the main employers in Perth and reflecting the accuracy of the early companies' assessment that Perth would be an important railway centre.

Perth contains some of the finest Georgian urban architecture in Scotland, the product of expansion and improvement begun when Thomas Hay Marshall was Lord Provost. One of these Georgian Streets, Marshall Place, built in the early 1800's, was named after him. It has a fine view looking south across the South Inch which could have been ruined if plans to site the railway station there had been carried out; the railway between the General Station and the Tay runs behind Marshall Place on an elevated track. The church with the distinctive crown steeple is Saint Leonard's in the Fields Free Church. It was built in 1885 on the site of the wooden hut that served as the studio of local photographic pioneer Magnus Jackson. He went on to better things, moving into new premises in Princes Street.

Marshall Place can be seen on the left of this view looking north along Princes Street. Like George Street and Saint John Street, it was made to connect the Edinburgh Road with the new Perth Bridge, cutting through the mediaeval burgh between South Street and Canal Street. When Queen Victoria passed through Perth in 1842 a triumphal arch was built at this South Inch end of Princes Street to greet her as she entered the town. The railway bridge had not yet been built, it followed a few years later when the Dundee and Perth Railway bridged the Tay to bring their rails into Perth. Their original station was Princes Street Station and a paling fence, part of the old station, can be seen running across the bridge here. When the new platforms were built at the General Station, Princes Street diminished in importance and is now disused.

'This is the German Gipsies at Perth taken on the South Inch', is the message written on the back of this old picture postcard published by local stationer J.S.Nicoll of South Methven Street. Even before the First World War these bands of wandering gipsies were universally unpopular in Britain. The South Inch is the smaller of the two remarkable areas of parkland that flank Perth. It used to extend up to the line of the old city walls at Canal Street, but over the years, the town encroached until it stopped at Marshall Place. The north east corner of the Inch was taken up in the 1650's by a citadel, one of four built in Scotland by Oliver Cromwell. It was occupied for less than ten years and quickly demolished after his death. The Pavilion Theatre, built on the site in 1928, was more popular, but it too has been knocked down.

Incessant rain for over a week, with only a few dry intervals, had people all over Perthshire cursing the vagiaries of the August weather in 1910. The rivers, unable to cope with such a deluge, rose to a climax with the high tides on the 29th causing widespread flooding. Some young men rowed one of the river hire boats around the North Inch, over the cricket pitch and round by Rose Terrace while another young man (it's always young men!) was seen bathing in the none too clean water flooding the South Inch. Children too enjoyed the sudden appearance of a new beach! Marshall Place, seen here, and the adjoining streets were all flooded to a depth of several inches. But, there's always a winner; this time it was the Corporation Tramways which saw a 20% rise in normal Monday revenue from people going to gawp at the floods.

When the apparently spring like conditions of mid-January 1918 were replaced by an intense frost, the Tay began to look like a serious threat to any river bourne Titanic. The river down to Perth was frozen from bank to bank and this picture from Moncrieffe Island shows the build up of ice below the railway bridge. In the background is the rotunda and chimney of the old water works, now used as a gallery dedicated to the artist, John Duncan Ferguson. The water supplies came from filter beds on Moncrieffe Island. The railway bridge was built in 1863 to replace the original which had been made of wood and was unsafe after only fourteen years. Before it was built, train passengers alighted at Barnhill and either crossed the Tay on a ferry, or took a coach over the Perth Bridge.

Elsewhere in Scotland the snow at Peterhead was 3 feet deep and trains in the Highlands were blocked in drifts, but there was great concern in Perth in case the ice built up around the bridges blocking the inevitable thaw and causing a flood, as had so often happened in the past. In the event it was the Annaty Burn in Scone that flooded (see page 41). Here the view shows Victoria Bridge with, to the left, the County Buildings, on the site of the old Gowrie House, and to the right, Tay Street with the steeple of Saint Matthew's church prominent against a glowering winter sky. Although the photographs on these two pages are uncredited they could be those advertised by W. B. McCallum of the Kodak Supply Stores, 8 Scott Street as 'just the thing to send your friends'. They were sold for two (old) pence each.

Floods are so much part of life in Perth that the levels of the worst floods are marked on the abutment of Perth Bridge beside the entrance to the North Inch; the highest was in 1814 when the ice-bound river blocked a rapid thaw. Such is the severity of these big floods that this innundation of 1912 not only does not merit a mark on the bridge, but inspired the local paper to suggest that '... a great deal of amusement was got from the the fact that the city was transformed into a kind of Venice' (!) Heavy rain and melting snow had combined to flood the North Inch up to the cannons in front of the Academy and surround the bandstand and monuments. The basements of houses in Rose Terrace and houses in the vicinity of North Port were also flooded. The great river continues to plague the people of Perth with disastrous floods.

When the floods recede the North Inch returns to pleasant and benign normality. This view from 1910 shows, on extreme left and right, the cannons set up in front of the Academy buildings in Rose Terrace. They are reputed to have been used in the Crimean War at the Battle of Sebastopol but both they and the railings surrounding them, were melted down to make shells for another, more recent, conflict. The obelisk in the distance, and surrounded by water on the previous page, was erected in honour of Lord Lyndoch and the Perthshire Volunteer Regiment (see page 35). But there is more to the North Inch than military memorials and clan battles. It is used for many sporting activities and is reputed to be where cricket was first played in Scotland, giving Perth a strong claim to be the home of Scottish cricket.

Atholl Street was part of Perth's Georgian New Town. This deserted scene (a flag day perhaps?) would be unthinkable today with traffic constantly on the move around the inner ring-road that Atholl Street now forms part of. At the corner of Atholl Street and Kinnoul Street was the old Theatre Royal. It was built in the 1820's and despite being thought too cramped for the major productions and too large for smaller shows it remained in use for over twenty years. A number of famous actors appeared there including Edmund Kean, who played Richard III to a packed house in 1822. The building of the Old City Hall appears to have hastened the demise of the Theatre which became a clothing workshop and warehouse. Despite its short life it is seen as a forerunner of the present Perth Theatre.

Residents in Barossa Place, at the edge of the North Inch, were (and probably still are) allowed to keep a couple of cows on the Inch. This street of delightful Regency villas was, in Georgian times, the northern limit of Perth. Here a delivery van of the City of Perth Co-operative Society Limited stands outside No.5 with the driver perched on top of an old Sunshine Soap box. The street was named after the Battle of Barossa, a Penninsular War encounter in which local hero, Thomas Graham, Lord Lyndoch, led a British force outnumbered by more than two to one, to victory against the French. He started soldiering late in life, after the death of his wife, and rose to the rank of General in Wellington's army. His regiment, the Perthshire Volunteers, later became the second battallion of the now disbanded Cameronians.

This shop at number 1 Main Street, Bridgend, on the corner with East Bridge Street, belonged to grocer and wine merchant David M Fisher. It is now the Bridgend Post Office and this view would be impossible today because a traffic light sits outside the front door and the road level has been raised giving the frontage a sunken appearance. Before the bridge was built Bridgend was a small village with a ferry house; and ferrymen. Their boats were small cobles (like that on page 54) which they rowed across the river. The original road running from Barnhill to Scone appears to have been on a lower level and so when the bridge was built roads were realigned and a new village emerged. The coming of the trams made a big difference too and encouraged housing development along the road between Bridgend and Scone.

The shop on the previous page is hidden behind the tram, here waiting for some cows to cross the bridge. The bridge was of great importance to the livestock markets in Perth because it gave farmers easier access than having to make their animals swim across the river between Kincarrathie and the North Inch. Before the days of motorised transport many beasts walked over the bridge to or from market, although these plodding animals seem to be in no hurry to go anywhere. When the bridge was first opened it was a toll bridge. The toll house is the small cottage-like building on the right. A replica sign from 1879, mounted on the front wall, describes the rules for the use of 'locomotives' on the bridge. The building half hidden by the toll house has now gone, but many more have been built on the hill above East Bridge Street.

Buses operated between Perth and Scone from the 1860's up to the 1890's when the bus company was taken over by the Perth and District Tramways Company Ltd. The horses that had hauled the buses were transferred to the trams but the fate of bus drivers, like Jamie here, is unclear. It would seem likely however that they too would have transferred to the trams with their teams. The tram service started in September 1895 and each tram had five teams of horses allocated to it; four working in shifts with one spare team. The depot and stables for the buses was in Scone and it too was taken over by the Tramways Company. The Tramways Company themselves were taken over by Perth Corporation in 1903 who replaced the horses two years later with faster and more frequent electric trams.

Most of the system was laid as single track with double railed passing places; these were extended when the system was electrified, but the overhead cables were double throughout the system, which helps to identify the direction trams are travelling in these old pictures. This tram is setting out on the standard route from Scone over Perth Bridge and through the town centre to Cherrybank. The long low building behind it is the depot which was converted for use by the electric trams. It is now used as a council recycling depot. The tram is passing the present day Scone Post Office and the local branch of the Bank of Scotland, but the shop on the left appears now to be a private dwelling. The pump in the foreground has also been superseded. The prominent steeple of Scone New Church can be seen in the distance.

The inhabitants of Old Scone were moved up the hill to New Scone by the Earl of Mansfield at the beginning of the eighteenth century, to improve his estate. The move was not the same as the infamous 'Highland clearances', but was perhaps more like the urban clearances of the 1960's when people were moved from inner cities to outlying suburbs; well meaning, but very distressing. Either way the new village appears to have been accepted by the inhabitants as a healthier place to live and has expanded considerably since its unpromising beginnings, much of the expansion coming as a result of the new tram services. These houses in Myrtle Road, at the northern end of the village, were built not long before this picture was taken in 1909 and bungalows were built in the 1930's at the edge of the field the horses are ploughing.

After two days of torrential rain in July 1916 the Annaty Burn could not contain the volume of water and overflowed, undermining the road and bringing down the front of these houses. The occupants had been taken to safety before the collapse, although some people had to be rescued when they stayed longer than was safe. When the wall came down several items of furniture, including a bed, fell into the burn and were washed away. The collapsed wall apparently created a breakwater which saved the next house. It had been built some years earlier to replace one that had itself been washed away when an ice spate crashed into it during a winter thaw. A similar spate sent huge blocks of ice into the houses when the burn flooded again after the severe frost that froze the Tay in January 1918 (see pages 30 and 31).

Cherrybank was a small country village until the Glasgow Road expanded out to it, encouraged by the tram service. Here a tram has arrived at the Cherrybank terminus from Scone. Behind it the road forks right to Stirling and the south, and left down the Low Road to Necessity Brae. Cherrybank School, founded in 1865, is obscured behind the gardens on the right. Cherrybank is now home to more than just suburban gardens. Five years after Arthur Bell and Sons moved into new offices at Cherrybank in the 1970's they began planting the Arthur Bell Garden. It was extended in 1984 as the Bell's Cherrybank Garden and further extended with Bell's National Heather Collection. The offices are now the commercial offices of United Distillers, while the gardens are one of the glories of Perth and known as Cherrybank Gardens.

Cherrybank was a 'tourist trap' long before the Cherrybank Gardens and again it was the trams that made it possible. Not only could people live in Cherrybank and work in town, but others could get out of town to visit the Buckie Braes, a wooded glen surrounding a branch of the Craigie Burn. Here some children strain to watch one of their pals sample the waters of Cock Robin's Well, one of the simple attractions of the 'Buckies' which included swings, a see-saw and, for those just a little bit older, lovers' walks through the secluded woods. They still exist, but Cock Robin's Well has lost its ladle, along with the magic it clearly once held. Above the Buckie Braes today is the new headquarters building of General Accident, set imaginatively into the hillside with roof gardens softening its impact on the landscape.

When this picture was taken, nearly a hundred years ago, it would have been impossible to believe that Perth's largest employer would one day be based out beyond these early developments along the Glasgow Road. This view across the Craigie Burn, from where the practice tee of the Craigie Hill Golf Course is now, shows the scattered beginnings of Glasgow Road and Viewlands. Viewlands Terrace can be seen leading off on the left of the picture and on the right is the 16th Century tower house Pitheavlis Castle, near the junction of Needless Road and Glasgow Road. The castle was home of the Oliphant family and their descendants for over three hundred years. The development of the area, initially encouraged by the trams, grew more rapidly when Perth Academy moved to Viewlands from Rose Terrace in 1932.

Like Viewlands, Burghmuir developed rapidly when the Academy moved out of the town centre. This view from the 1930's shows Burghmuir Road looking down to its junction with Letham Road and Jeanfield Road from the point where Fairies Road joins from the right. The largely unmade road and footpaths, and the absence of trees in the gardens, shows how new the development was when the picture was taken. At one time the Muir was covered by extensive woods, but these were felled over time to provide firewood until by the early nineteenth century few trees remained. Paths through the woods provided popular walks and it is likely that Fairies Road was one of these. It was still a country path, believed to be the haunt of fairies, before its magic was swamped by housing, cars and tarmac. But maybe still, at midnight, in the moonlight ...

The tram terminus was at the junction of Dunkeld Road and Crieff Road; the tram here is about to set off for the Cross at the foot of High Street. Just out of picture on the left is the Northern District School. The houses on the left are now adorned by a forest of bed and breakfast signs. In the distance, to the right of the tram, is the Wallace Linen Works built in 1868 for John Shields and Co. They wove fine linen damask; so fine that Perth gave a wedding present of their table linens to King George V and Queen Mary. The works started with 300 looms which had increased to 900 by the turn of the century. There were many sports facilities in Dunkeld Road, the swimming baths, the Ice Rink, home of the one time Perth Panthers ice hockey team and beside it Saint Johnstone Football Club's old Muirton Park ground.

Perth had a number of early football teams, but it was some time before one of them, Saint Johnstone, became the town's senior team. The club was formed in 1884 playing its early games at the Recreation Ground off the Edinburgh Road. It became a member of the Scottish Football League in 1911, was promoted to the first division in 1924 and opened the new ground at Muirton on Christmas Day that year. The record crowd there was 29,972 for a game against Dundee in 1952, but it was to accommodate those crowds in greater comfort and safety that the club moved to the new all-seater stadium of McDiarmid Park in 1989. This team for the 1935/36 season was, left to right, back row: Welsh, Clark, Wyllie, Baxter, Littlejohn and Smeaton: front Row: Tennant, Adam, Lyle, Ferguson (capt.) and Nicholson.

The Dunkeld Road to Craigie tram route passed under King Street Bridge and so three trams, numbers 10,11 and 12, were built three inches lower and painted a different colour than the others. Ironically the Caledonian Railway raised the bridge in 1907 making the distinction no longer necessary. Here, in this picture from 1906, number 11 has just crossed Saint Leonard's bridge and is heading down Priory Place; the carters on the right appear to be holding back their horses to let it pass. The double tracks here became a single track at the Craigie terminus at the end of Priory Place. Behind the tram is the Craigie Post Office, but now an adjacent cafe building partially obscures the distant view of the General Station tower. The picture also predates the distinctive Craigie clock.

Priory Place can be seen on the extreme left of this picture of Carr's Croft. The street named Carr's Croft today runs off Priory Place at right angles to it although these old cottages facing Priory Place were also known as Carr's Croft. The front of one cottage still survives, as a plumbers showroom. The thatched roof has been replaced by corrugated iron, but there is still a section of cobbled footpath in front of it. The modern Priory Place road can be seen on the extreme left of the picture, it has been elevated above the original ground level so that horse drawn vehicles, including trams, could cross the Saint Leonards bridge over the railway. It is hidden behind the cottages. The modern shops in the left background are still there, with a joinery contractors yard between them and the one surviving cottage.

To Dundonians of a criminal persuasion a trip 'up the river' means an involuntary stay at Perth Prison; one of the ten largest employers in the town. The site was originally a prisoner of war camp, or depot, for French prisoners during the Napoleonic wars. It was apparently a hellish place where thousands of men were kept in dreadful conditions. They were allowed to make trinkets which they sold to local people at a market, where they could also buy provisions. Many men escaped, but many died here, miles from home. In the 1970's some of their graves were unearthed during construction work and are now commemorated by a plaque. The present prison was opened on the site many years after the War and holds considerably fewer prisoners than the miserable French, whose only crime had been to fight for their country.

Perth's position in the centre of the country on a navigable river must have made it as important to early shipping as it later was to the railways. It was apparently possible at one time to navigate as far up river as Old Scone, but most early trade was to quays beside the mediaeval burgh. Gradual silting of the river however and the increase in the size of boats meant that the quays moved down to beside the South Inch and gradually further down river until now the harbour is concentrated here at Friarton. The wooden piled wharves seen in this picture have been replaced by steel and concrete although the cargoes they handled have changed little over the years with building materials, coal and fertilisers coming in and stone, timber and agricultural produce going out. The volume of trade however has increased significantly in recent years.

The kind of vessels using the Tay over the centuries have varied in size from prehistoric dug out canoes to large modern coasters carrying huge tonnages. These puffers photographed on the Tay are typical of early twentieth century coastal traffic. Puffers are more usually associated with the west coast, but many worked out of east coast ports as well. Some of them were requisitioned by the Admiralty during World War 1 and astonishingly were to be found operating as fleet tenders during the Battle of Jutland. Steam power was an important innovation for a tidal, river harbour like Perth, because ships were no longer at the mercy of the elements. Most vessels using the harbour now are European; some equipped to travel many more miles inland on continental waterways than the mere thirty miles from the sea to Perth.

Tay pleasure steamers operated mainly between Perth and Dundee calling at riverside piers at Bridge of Earn, Newburgh and Balmerino. The larger paddle steamers, like the Marchioness of Bute (on the front cover), also cruised outside the Tay estuary to Saint Andrews, Arbroath, Montrose and round the Bell Rock. One of the smaller steamers, the Star o' Tay, went the other way, with masts and funnel hinged she sailed past Perth Bridge and apparently attempted to go as far as Scone Palace. Most steamers were requisitioned for Admiralty service during the First World War and the service never recovered, although one that did manage to keep going after the War was the Cleopatra. She is seen here leaving Perth on one of her regular downriver cruises to Newburgh and Dundee. She ceased cruising in the 1930's.

Salmon Fishing on the Tay—Shipping Nets. 970

The Tay is perhaps better known for its salmon than its shipping and salmon fishermen, concerned about possible damage to their livelihood, apparently objected to plans to 'improve' the navigable channel in the mid nineteenth century. For centuries, during the season from February to August, hundreds of men worked out of numerous fishing stations on both banks of the river. They worked with hand knitted nets and small cobles like this, but catches have dwindled in recent years due to the activities of sea fishermen. London was the main market; before the railway, boats sailed regularly during the season with fish packed in ice, saved during the winter from special ponds. Another fish caught on the Tay was the sparling which has a curious smell, like cucumber. There was sometimes considerable rivalry between the two fisheries.

I started with a puzzle (page 2) and end with one: what is this shed like structure for loading railway trucks, is it associated with the old Friarton Gas Works, or the quarries and is it, as it appears to be, in the cutting at the northern end of Moncrieffe Tunnel? Before the Scottish Central Railway could bring their trains into Perth they first had to cut the Moncrieffe Tunnel which at over 1200 yards was the fifth longest tunnel in Scotland. It was also soon being used by the Edinburgh and Northern Railway which had running powers over the Scottish Central's tracks from Hilton Junction. Three air shafts on top of the hill ventilate the tunnel, one can just be seen in the distance on the right on the very edge of picture. Perth's only real brush with the enemy during the Second World War was when a German bomb landed near the tunnel in 1940.

BIBLIOGRAPHY

George Penny	Traditions of Perth 1836: re-print by Culross 1986.
David Graham-Campbell	Perth - The Fair City: John Donald 1994.
Marion L. Stavert	Perth - A Short History: Perth and Kinross District Libraries 1991.
John Aitken	Above the Tay Bridges: John Aitken and John Normand 1986.
Perthshire Advertiser	Know Your Perth: two volumes 1980's.
Roy Boutcher & William Kemp	The Theatre in Perth: Perth Theatre 1975.
Scone Community Council	New Scone - The By-gone Life.
Perth Civic Trust	series of leaflets on old Perth.
Lin Collis	Reflections of Old Perth: Perth Museum and Art Gallery.
Graham Ogilvy	The River Tay and its People: Mainstream Publishing Co. 1993.
Alan W.Brotchie	Tramways of the Tay Valley: Dundee Museum and Art Gallery 1965.
Marie Weir	Ferries in Scotland: John Donald 1988.

ACKNOWLEDGEMENTS

I would like to thank the many people of Perth who so cheerfully and courteously helped me when I stopped them to ask for information. I will always think of their kindness and generosity as typical of Perth. I enjoyed using the excellent new facilities at the A.K.Bell library as well as the more familiar ones at the Mitchell Library in Glasgow. I would like to thank Perth Theatre for the picture on page 16; despite what I say in the text, it revived a very pleasant childhood memory. I should also thank the usually anonymous people who have so liberally scattered interpretive panels around the town; they are excellent and very informative.

York Place at the junction with Caledonian Road about 1900.